BUILDING THE WORLD

TRANSPORTATION

PAUL MASON

PowerKiDS press

Published in 2024 by The Rosen Publishing Group, Inc.
2544 Clinton Street, Buffalo, NY 14224

First published in Great Britain in 2019 by Wayland

Series editor: Julia Bird
Produced by Tall Tree Ltd
Editor: Jon Richards
Designer: Ed Simkins

Cataloging-in-Publication Data

Names: Mason, Paul.
Title: Transportation/ Paul Mason.
Description: New York : Powerkids Press, 2024. | Series: Building the world | Includes glossary, index and bibliographic information.
Identifiers: ISBN 9781642827385 (pbk) | ISBN 9781642827392 (library bound) | ISBN 9781642827408 (ebook)
Subjects: LCSH: Air travel--Juvenile literature | Emergency vehicles-- Juvenile literature |Public transportation--Juvenile literature | Traffic engineering--Juvenile literature | Transportation--Juvenile literature
Classification: LCC TA1149 M37 2024 | DDC 629.04--dc23

Picture credits: Dreamstime: 10l, 10t, 10b, 11t, 11tc, 10-11, 31c Sentavio, Shutterstock: 1bl Treter, 1c naulicrea, 1tr, 2t, 27tr Lytvynova Alina, 1br GoodStudio, 4t EvrenKalinbacak, 4-5b Sakarin Sawasdinaka, 5tr Everett Historical, 2cl, 7b, 15b, 18-19, 31b, 32r Macrovector, 2c, 6-7, 6tl, 7cr, 14tl, 15cr, 26cl, 30 Golden Sikorka, 2b, 14b VectorPot, 6cl 3t0n4k, 6bl vectorpouch, 7t Siberian Art, 8bl Marc Bruxelle, 8br DW labs Incorporated, 9t Kong_Setthavaut, 9r Kevin J. Frost, 12br Plamen Galabov, 13b Angelo Giampiccolo, 14-15 tele52, 15t Alfazet Chronicles, 16cr cyo bo, 16-17 CIS, 17c A. Aleksandravicius, 17b Rhonda Roth, 18-19 Treter, 20-21 Roberto Sorin, 22c naulicrea, 22b, 23t, 23b aurielaki, 24l MoonRock, 24br Rocky Grimes, 24-25 Phil Whitten, 25tr Mascha Tace, 26tl Hilch, 26-27 Sentavio, 27b Dilen, 28bl Robert Gubbins, 29t Frederic Legrand – COMEO, 29c Igor Karasi, Creative Commons: 12bl Library of Congress, 20b Brittany Ferries, 21t Siemens AG, 25br Sdlewis, 28t Theodor Horydczak

Manufactured in the United States of America
CPSIA Compliance Information: Batch #CSPK24. For further information contact Rosen Publishing at 1-800-237-9932.

CONTENTS

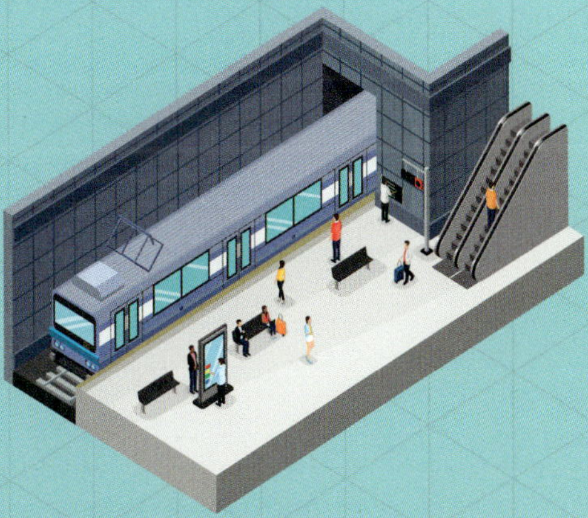

Moving people, *MOVING THINGS*

Where we live, our jobs, where we go to school, and even what we eat are all linked by the transport system. Our world would be very different without it.

Moving people

We use two main kinds of transportation to move from place to place. The first is personal transportation, which includes cars, motorcycles, and bicycles. Owning your own transportation is convenient – but it is also expensive and can cause lots of pollution. Public transportation can carry a much larger number of people efficiently, causing less pollution. Public transportation includes buses, trams, and trains.

Shinkansen, or bullet trains, are very fast trains that travel through Japan at speeds of more than 186 mph (300 kph).

Moving things

Many different kinds of transport are used to move goods around – carrying anything from new cars to lettuce. Trucks, boats, and airplanes can all carry a lot of items, including cargo and people. In crowded cities, smaller vehicles such as delivery vans, scooters, and bicycles are often used to make deliveries.

Around 80 percent of goods are transported by container ship.

Horse-drawn carts and airships, such as this one flying over New York City, are modes of transport that have nearly disappeared today.

Changing technologies

Transport is constantly changing as new technologies develop. After 100 years of cars that use diesel- or gas-powered engines, electric vehicles are now becoming more common. New technologies, such as satellite navigation, tracking systems, and smartphone apps, are also changing the ways we use transport.

1.674 billion

People transported by air in 2000 and 2017

3.979 billion

Traffic
TROUBLE

Our streets are busy with all kinds of vehicles. They are so busy that in some cities, the amount of traffic causes problems. New technology is helping to solve these.

Traffic management

Traffic cameras watch places that are especially busy. They can spot when there are lots of cars and people and then manage the flow of traffic by changing traffic lights or adjusting speed limits. Computers in people's cars also warn them about traffic jams and suggest different routes.

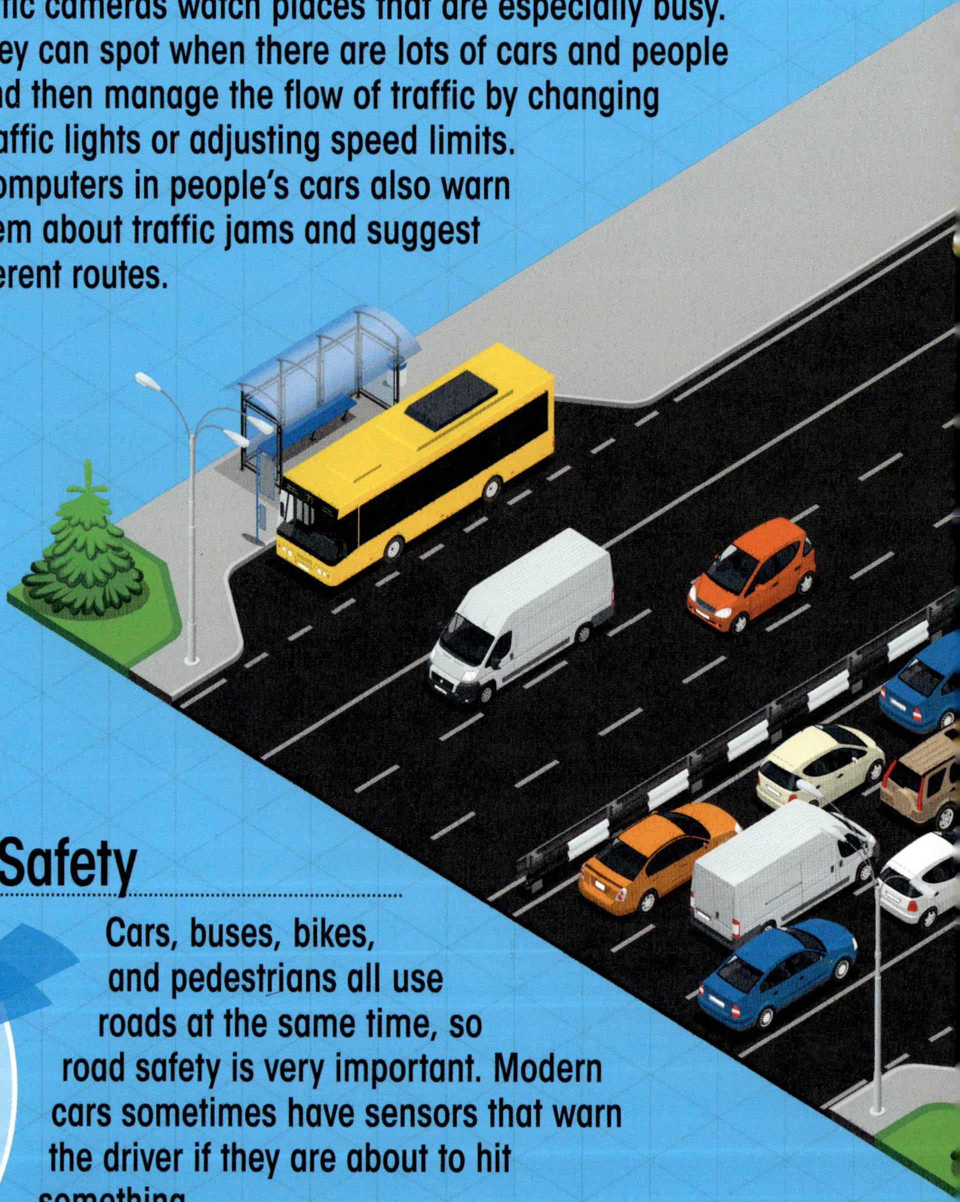

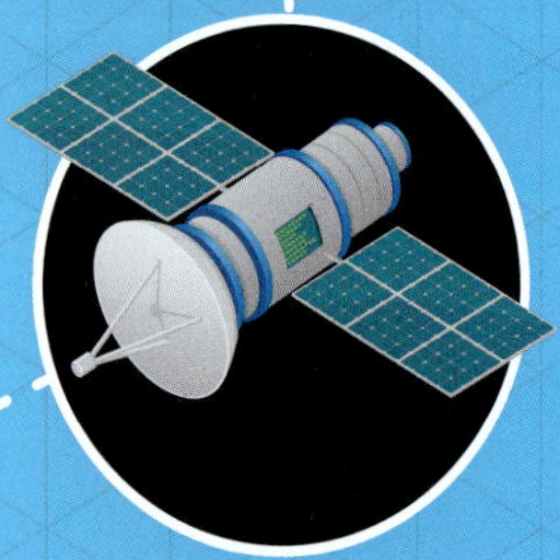

Signals from satellites in space tell a car's computer exactly where it is.

Safety

Cars, buses, bikes, and pedestrians all use roads at the same time, so road safety is very important. Modern cars sometimes have sensors that warn the driver if they are about to hit something.

Pulses of sound bounce off objects and back to the car's sensor, telling it if there is something in the way.

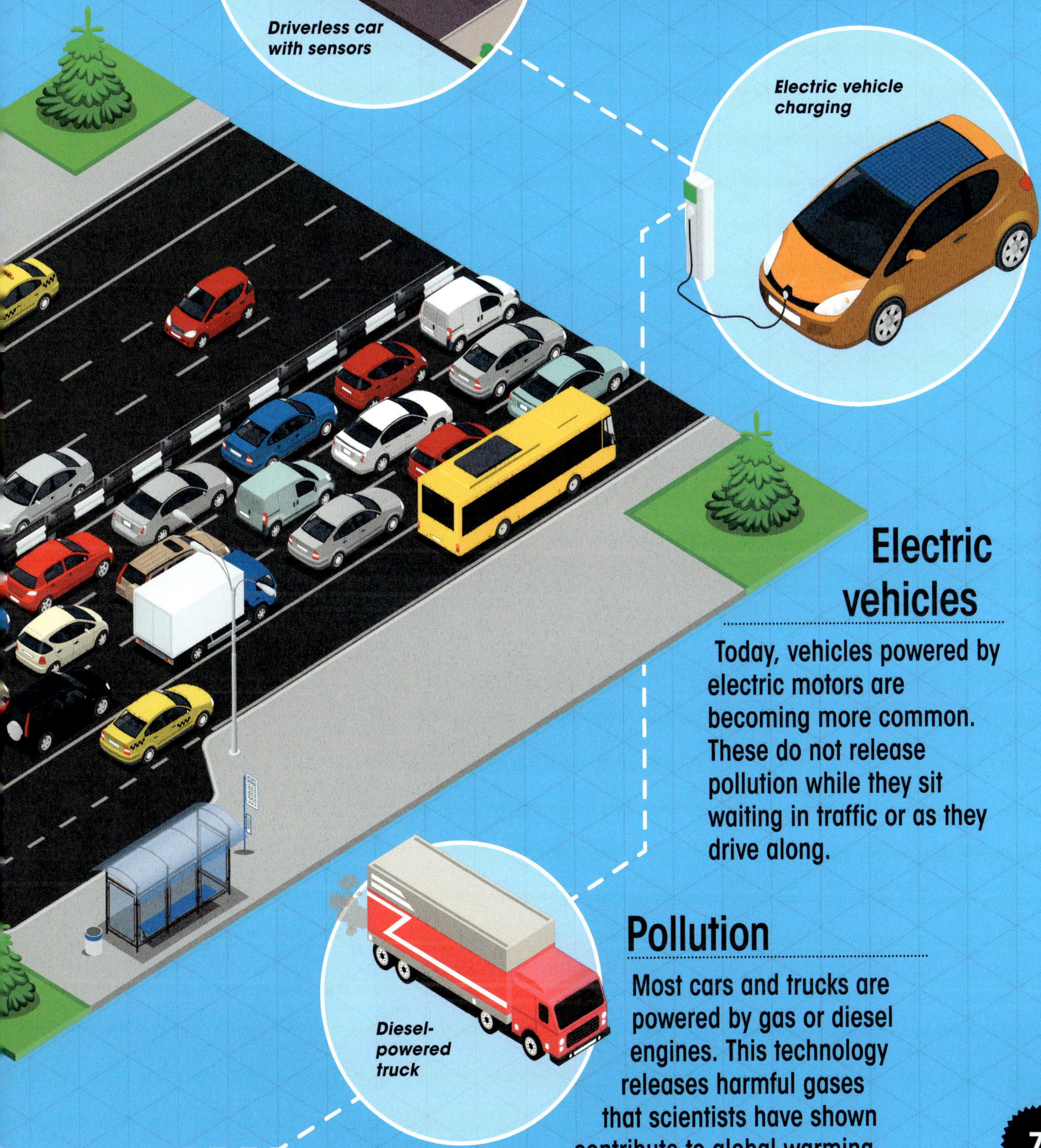

Driverless cars

Cars are being developed that do not need a driver. Computers on board the car use satellite navigation, sensors, and cameras to steer it without hitting anything.

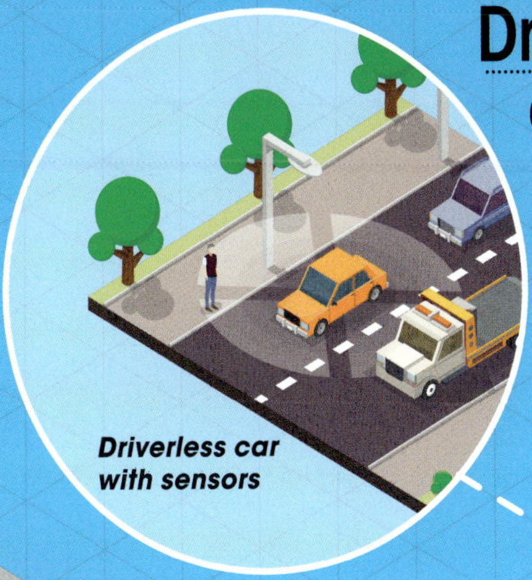

Driverless car with sensors

Electric vehicle charging

Electric vehicles

Today, vehicles powered by electric motors are becoming more common. These do not release pollution while they sit waiting in traffic or as they drive along.

Diesel-powered truck

Pollution

Most cars and trucks are powered by gas or diesel engines. This technology releases harmful gases that scientists have shown contribute to global warming.

Cars and *TRUCKS*

Cars are still one of the most popular ways for people to travel, while most food and goods are delivered by truck. The number of cars and trucks on the roads grows every year.

Number of cars in use around the world:

775,573,000

947,080,000

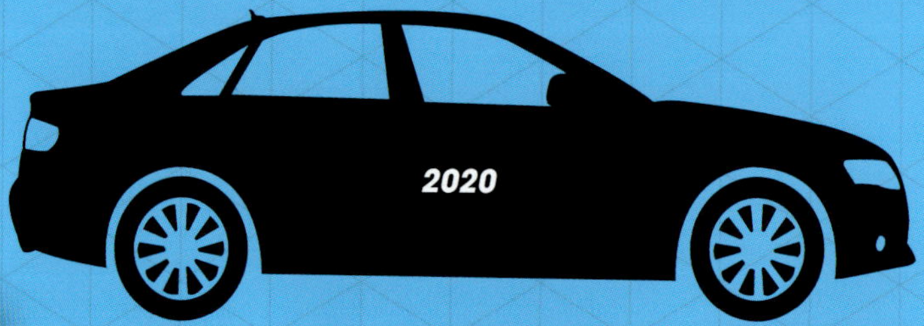

>1 billion

Road damage

The rise in vehicle numbers is affecting roads. Heavy trucks and lots of cars cause the road surface to break down. Potholes appear – some are big enough for a car wheel to drop into!

Once a road is damaged, cold weather makes the hole worsen until it is repaired.

Buses and trams cause less damage to the road per passenger than cars.

Singapore was the first city in the world to introduce a congestion charge.

Congestion charging

A congestion charge is money drivers have to pay for entering a city in their car or truck. It is a way of reducing congestion and pollution by cutting down the number of vehicles on the streets. Today, cities including London, Milan, San Diego, and Stockholm charge for vehicles to drive in them.

ANPR systems

Congestion charging uses a system called Automatic Number Plate Recognition, or ANPR. First, cameras record the registration number of the car. They send this information to a computer database. This tells them details of the owner. If the owner has not paid the congestion charge, they are fined.

Fully electric vehicles do not have to pay a congestion charge because they produce less pollution. Numbers of electric and hybrid cars are predicted to keep growing:

2018 **6 million**

2022 **25 million**

2026 **60 million**

2030 **127 million**

Inside an *AIRPORT*

The biggest airports are designed to handle millions of people every year. All these passengers have security checks to pass before they can board a plane. Many have luggage to check in too.

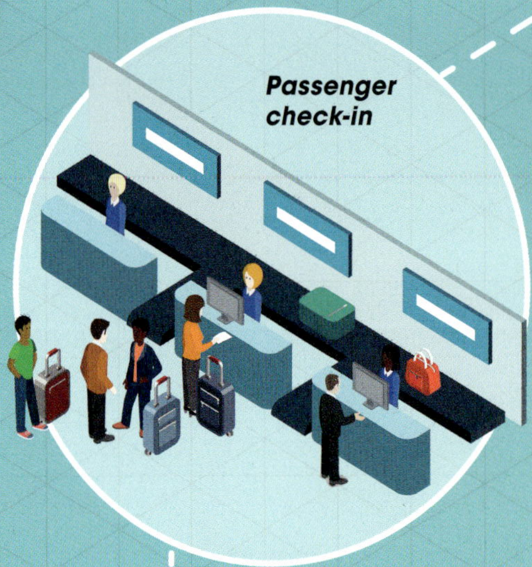

Check-in

This is where passengers can confirm their flight and seat, and drop their luggage to be put into the plane's hold.

Transport links

Most large airports are located outside cities where there is room to build runways and terminal buildings. In order for passengers to reach or leave the airport, there needs to be a network of transport links, such as roads, railways, and even boat services.

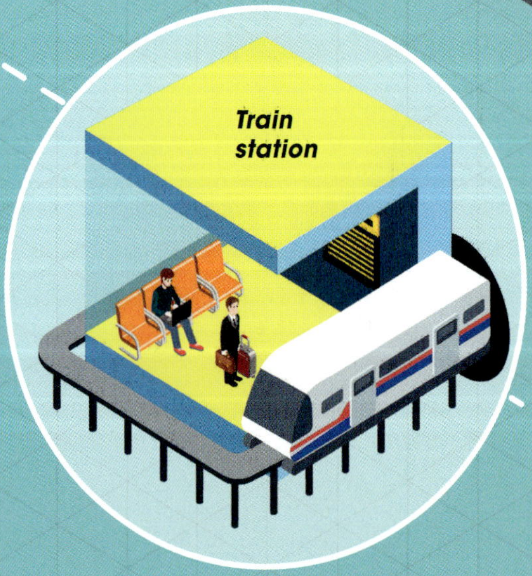

Security and passport control

Departing passengers have to pass through security checks to make sure that they are not carrying dangerous items. Arriving passengers have their documents checked at passport control.

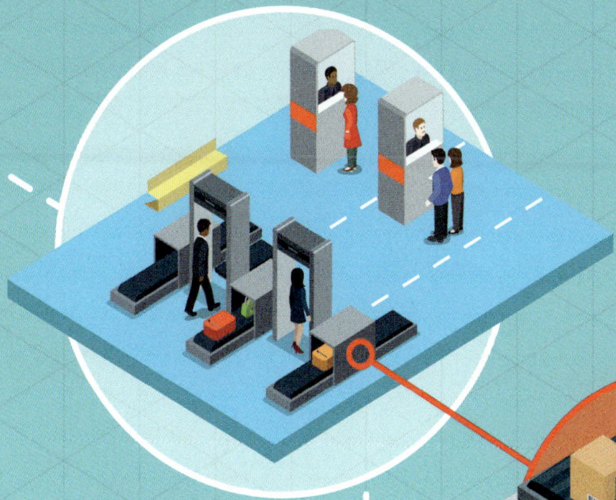

Passengers walk through detectors before boarding.

Luggage and cargo are checked using X-ray machines.

Waiting lounge

After passing through security checks, passengers can wait for their flight in the lounge where there are usually shops and restaurants.

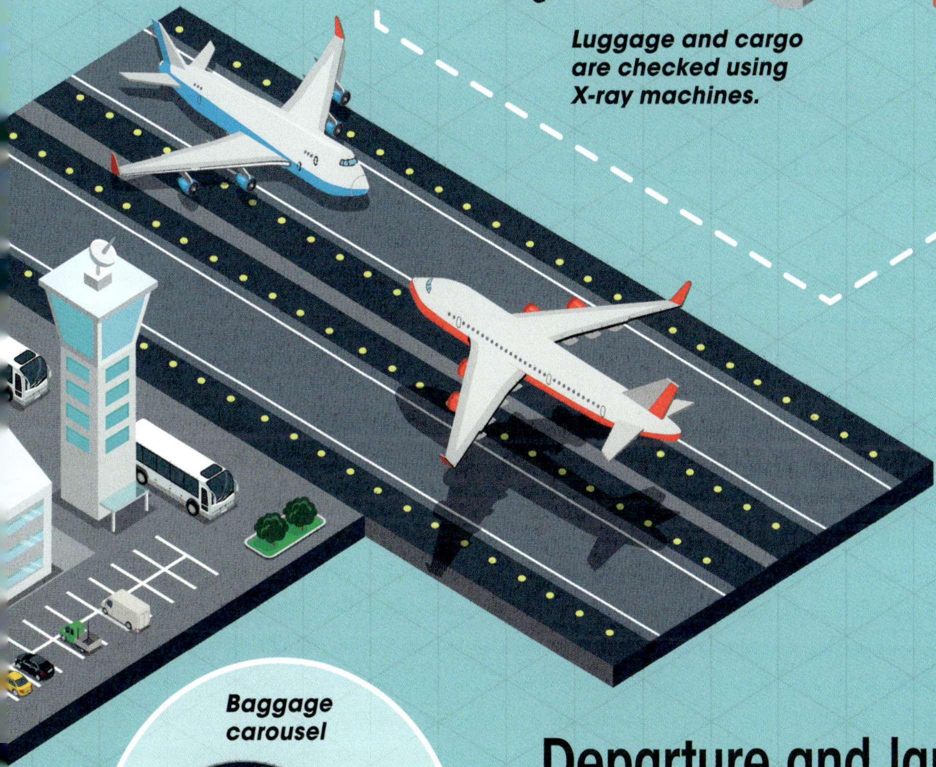

Departure and landing

Planes arrive and take off from the airport's runway. Arriving passengers leave the plane and enter the terminal building.

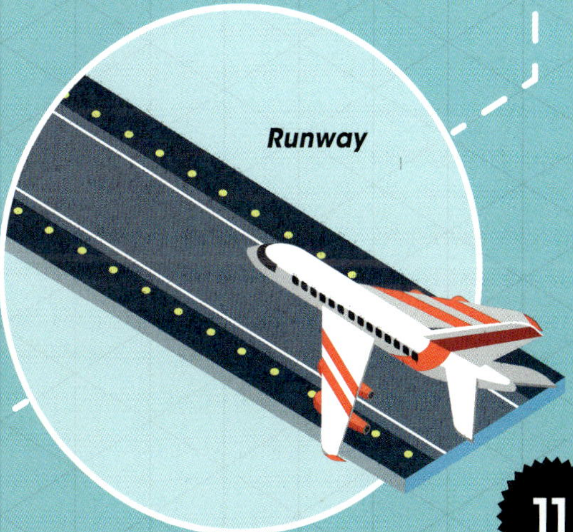

Baggage claim

Passengers collect their luggage from baggage carousels before passing through customs.

Moving people THROUGH THE AIR

On December 10, 1913, the first ever passenger flight took off in Russia. The plane was a Sikorsky Ilya Muromets, with 16 people aboard. Ever since, planes have been carrying people around the world.

In 2017, about

4.1 billion

people took commercial flights around the globe, up from

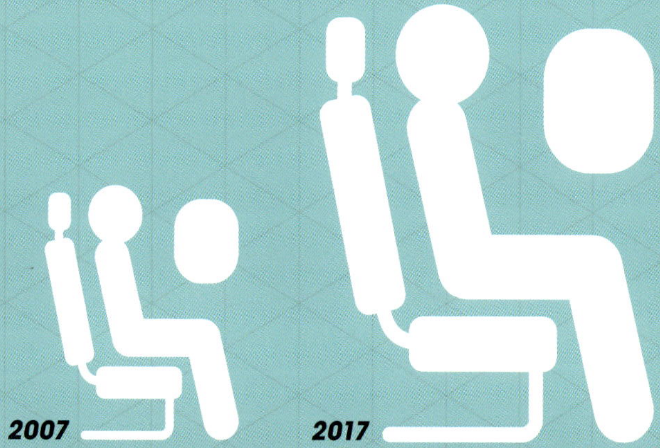

2.456 billion

people in 2007.

Early airports

The first airports were just big fields with flat surfaces. Once planes started carrying passengers, though, airports became more luxurious. The wealthy people who could afford to fly did not want to wait for their transportation in a field!

This U.S. airport (above) from the 1940s looks very different from today's modern airports, such as this one in Dubai, UAE (right).

The 1952 De Havilland Comet (above) was the world's first passenger jet "airliner." Jet power made planes much faster than before.

Jet power

In the 1950s, passenger planes started to use jet engines. These suck air into the front of the engine using a fan. The air is squeezed into a narrow space, mixed with fuel, and set alight. Jets of propelling gas shoot backward, pushing the plane forward.

Controlling the skies

With so many planes in the air, someone has to make sure they do not crash into each other. This is the job of air traffic controllers. They use radar and computers to keep the skies safe.

Computer screens show airplane locations to air traffic controllers.

Public
TRANSPORT

Public transport is a network of vehicles in which anyone can travel. By changing between different vehicles - from train to bus, for example - a traveler can get within walking distance of most destinations.

Long-distance trains

Long-distance trains link cities (and sometimes countries) together. There is usually no need to check in or go through passport control. They can sometimes be faster than traveling by air.

The world's fastest passenger train service travels between Shanghai Airport and the city of Shanghai. It travels 18.6 miles (30 km) in seven minutes.

Local trains

Local trains are slower and stop more often than long-distance ones. In cities, some run above the streets: these are called elevated railways. Others run through underground tunnels.

Travel information

Display screens at the station tell travelers when trains are arriving or leaving. Outside at the bus stop, smaller boards show when the next bus is due. Sometimes you can use an app to get the same information sent straight to your smartphone.

In 2011, three friends began a 43,208-mile (69,537 km) tour in their London taxi cab. They kept the meter running during the 15-month trip for a fare of nearly £80,000!

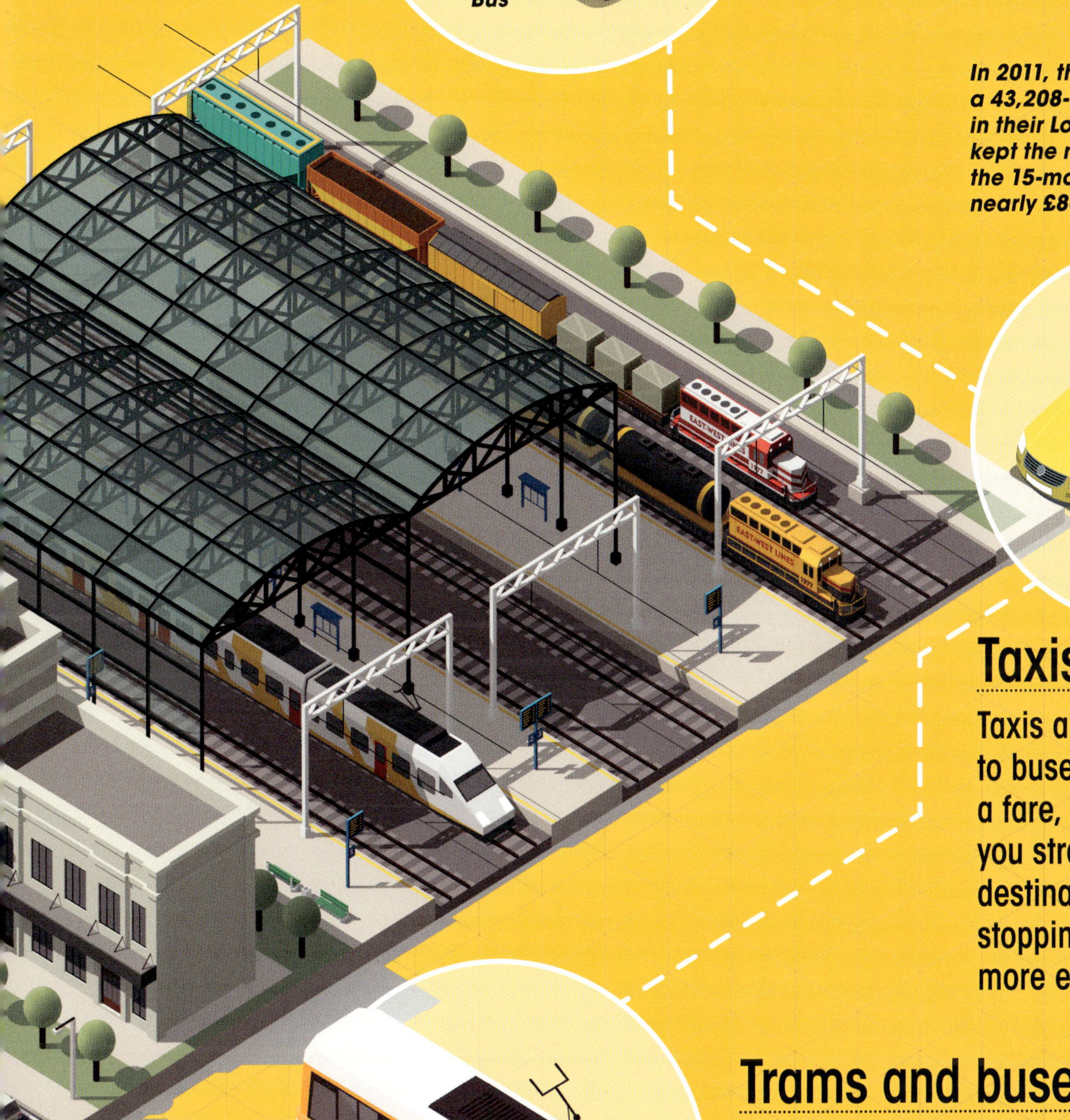

Taxis

Taxis are an alternative to buses or trams. For a fare, they can take you straight to your destination without stopping, but they are more expensive to use.

Trams and buses

To or from the train station, travelers can catch a tram or bus. Trams can only follow a set route, but buses can go almost anywhere. Some buses are large, such as an 80-passenger double-decker; others carry half as many people.

Trains, trams, AND BUSES

With the development of technology, modern public transport enables passengers to travel more quickly and conveniently than ever before.

High-speed trains

Some trains use technology to travel at hundreds of miles (km) an hour. They are designed with an aerodynamic shape, which slips easily through the air. The rails are one long piece of metal, without gaps like the rails normal trains run along. This reduces vibration, which at high speed could derail the train. The route is as straight as possible so that the train can maintain its speed.

Maglev

Some trains are powered by a system called maglev, which is short for "magnetic levitation." Powerful magnets lift the train above the track, so that it hovers there, not touching the rails. Other magnets shoot the train forward, pushing it to speeds of more than 372 mph (600 kph).

Maglev trains can reach incredibly high speeds because they do not experience friction from wheels running against rails.

The TGV (Train à Grande Vitesse) is a high-speed train network running through France.

Driverless trains

Some trains run without a driver at the controls. Computers and sensors control the train's speed, its stops, and when doors open and close. Sensors in the doors act much like an elevator door, preventing passengers from getting trapped.

Driverless trains operate in São Paulo, Miami, Hong Kong, Singapore, Paris, London, and many other big cities.

In Europe, trains and trams together provide **45%** of public transport.

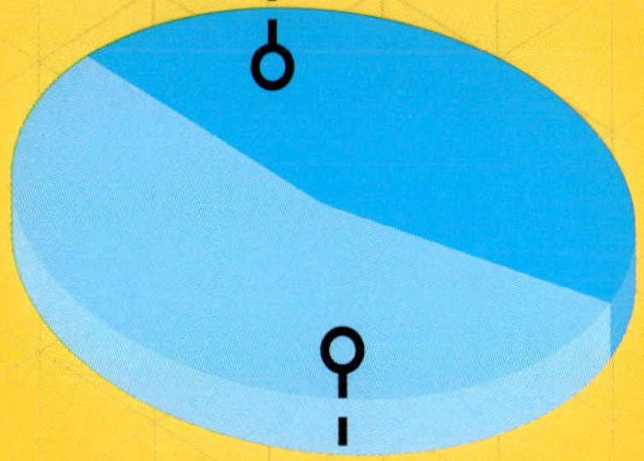

Buses and coaches provide **55%** of public transport.

In some cities, buses are powered by hydrogen, which does not pollute the air.

The environment

In general, public transport is better for the environment than private transport. This is because each vehicle carries more people, so the amount of pollution released per person is lower. Electric-powered public transport is even cleaner.

At the *HARBOR*

At a busy harbor, you can spot all kinds and sizes of ships. Some are cargo ships for carrying goods. Others are for carrying passengers, or for just having fun on the water.

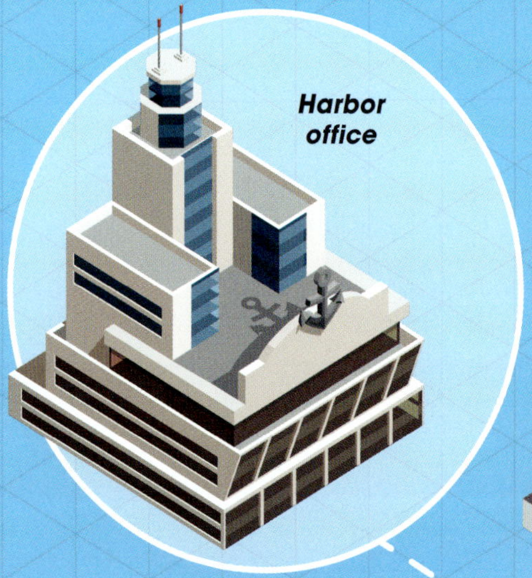

Traffic management

Ships cannot just come straight to dock as soon as they arrive at a harbor. The harbor office controls when ships come in and which ones have to wait out on the water.

At any one time, about 55,000 container ships are traveling the world's oceans, transporting goods.

Container ships

These huge ships transport many of the world's goods from country to country. Toys or computers made in China, for example, travel to the rest of the world on container ships.

Cruise ships

Cruise ships are like huge floating hotels that transport vacationers from place to place in comfort.

Tugs

These little boats have powerful engines. They can tow even the largest ships safely out of port, where there is deeper water and room for them to maneuver.

Loading

Containers are loaded aboard ships using cranes. In the port office, the loading is controlled by computers, which keep track of which container has been loaded aboard each ship.

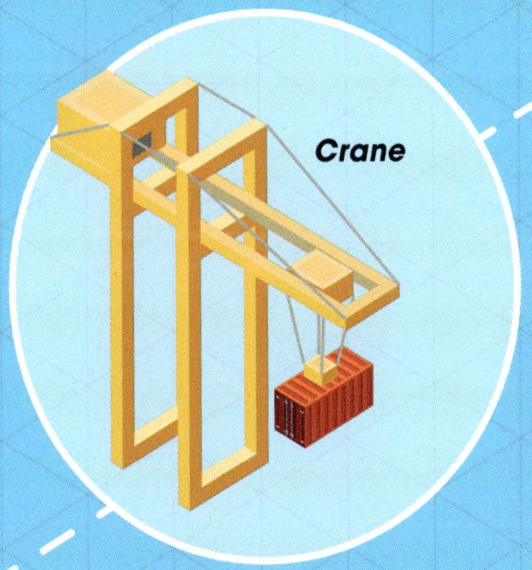

Most containers are fitted with a tracking tag. The container's exact location can be found using Global Positioning System (or GPS) - the same system a car's sat-nav uses (see pages 6-7).

Big-ship *TECHNOLOGY*

Most of the world's goods are transported by ship. Shipbuilders and owners are constantly trying to come up with new technology to make their ships better.

Most ships use diesel oil as fuel. This has a big effect on the environment. In fact, if shipping was a country, it would be the world's

SIXTH-BIGGEST

producer of carbon emissions.

Alternative fuels

Some ships now use alternative fuel technology. The ferry *Honfleur* (below) is designed to carry passengers and goods across the English Channel. It is powered by natural gas, which causes less pollution than diesel oil. A few other ships now use a combination of diesel and electricity.

Cruise ship tech

Some modern cruise ships are loaded with technology, including:

- Interactive digital signs that help passengers find their way. One cruise ship even uses a robot to give directions.
- Electronic bracelets passengers can use to open their door, order food and drink, and get on and off the ship.
- Geolocation bracelets for children, which let parents see on a computer screen exactly where their kids are.

Azimuth thrusters

One problem with big ships is how to steer them safely into port. Azimuth thrusters have been developed as an alternative to tugs (see page 19). These are pods with a propeller inside. The pod can change direction, like a ship's rudder. They make it possible to steer a huge ship around a tight bend, or even sideways toward a dock.

These giant azimuth thrusters (above) can be moved around to steer a ship in different directions.

Cruise ships like this are designed to be as light as possible. The higher up you go, the lighter the materials must be to avoid it being top heavy.

2009
17.8 million

2014
22.34 million

2019
29.7 million

The number of passengers on cruise ships worldwide.

Emergency *TRANSPORT*

Reaching an emergency in time to save lives or prevent crimes needs specialist vehicles. These are designed to carry trained people and equipment quickly and safely.

Emergency calls

In many countries, people can dial a phone number for emergency help. The operator asks where they are and which emergency service they need. The caller is put through to the relevant service.

If you dial the emergency number from a mobile phone, in some countries the operator can tell roughly where you are from which mobile phone tower is nearest to you.

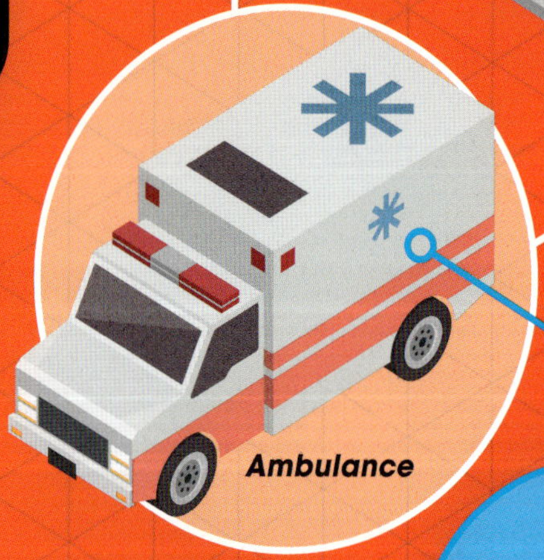

If an emergency vehicle appears, other vehicles must pull to the side of the road and let it pass.

Ambulances

Ambulances carry drugs and medical equipment for treating patients before they arrive at the hospital. The ambulance is usually crewed by two trained paramedics.

The Italian police's super-fast Lamborghini Huracán is used for catching speeders and transporting emergency medical supplies.

Police cars

Police cars are usually either patrol cars or pursuit cars. Both have a siren, emergency lights and a radio, and often a computer. The computer is linked to a police database which gives information about crimes and criminals.

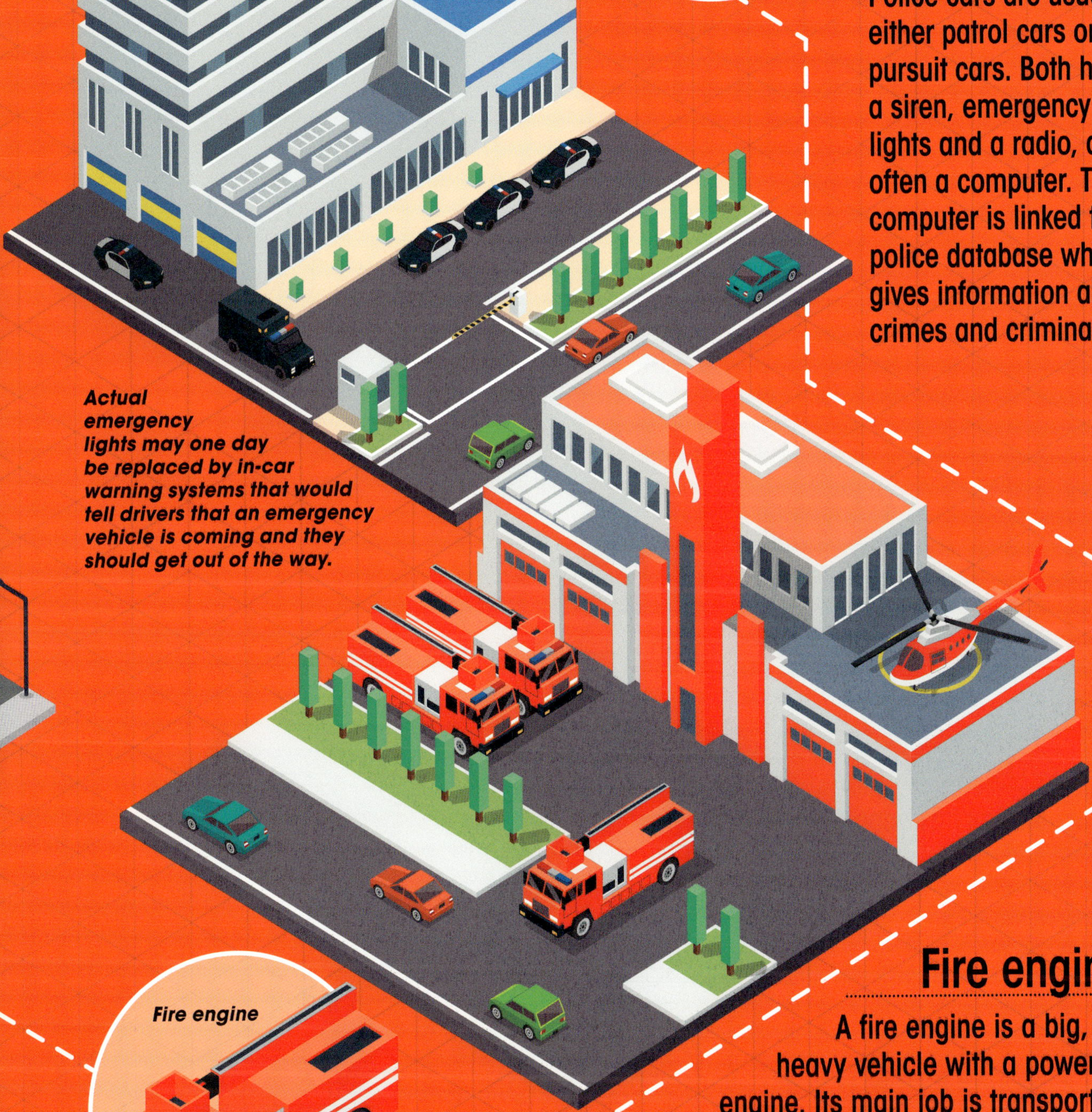

Actual emergency lights may one day be replaced by in-car warning systems that would tell drivers that an emergency vehicle is coming and they should get out of the way.

Fire engine

A fire engine is a big, heavy vehicle with a powerful engine. Its main job is transporting firefighters and their equipment, including ladders, hoses, and pumps. The vehicle may also contain a large tank full of water to fight the fire.

Emergency VEHICLES

Most of us have seen police cars, fire engines, and ambulances on the road. Here are some technology-loaded emergency vehicles that you might not have seen before.

The average number of calls each year for emergency medical services in the U.S.

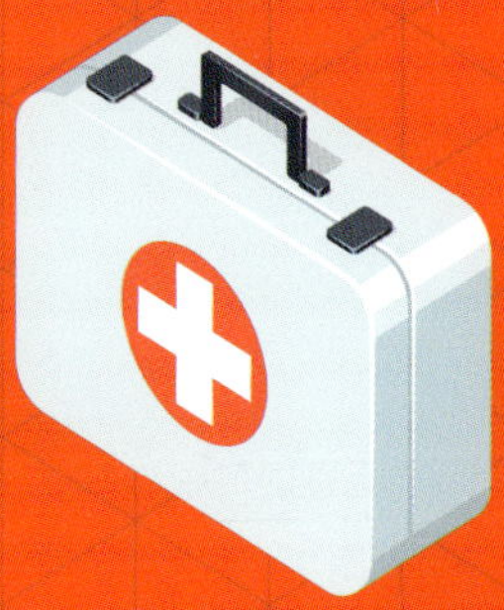

240 million

Coast guards carry out search and rescue operations, and investigate illegal shipping activities.

Coast guard

Countries have coast guards that handle emergencies at sea. They have many types of vehicles, from icebreaker ships in cold areas to surveillance aircraft. For chasing criminals, the U.S. Coast Guard has high-speed pursuit boats with powerful engines that can push the boats to 60 mph (100 kph). They are fitted with shock-absorbing seats for the crew, who get bounced around on the waves. The boats are self-righting if they get turned over.

67 *The number of different airplanes used by the Royal Flying Doctor Service to provide medical care and ambulance services in remote parts of Australia.*

Air ambulance

An air ambulance is a helicopter. It is used for accidents in places where a normal ambulance could not reach, or when a casualty has to be moved very fast. In London, new technology is helping the air ambulance get airborne faster. A new app sends the location of an accident to the pilot. This gets the ambulance airborne up to two minutes faster – which could save someone's life.

SWAT response

SWAT stands for Special Weapons and Tactics. American SWAT police officers confront criminals who are likely to be heavily armed. They sometimes have to use bulletproof vehicles during their work. One of the most popular is the Lenco Bearcat. It is covered in steel armor, has bulletproof glass, and the tires will not go down if they are shot.

Cleaner
AIR

Car manufacturers are moving away from diesel and gas-powered cars, which pollute the air and produce gases that cause climate change. Many new cars are powered by "clean" electrical motors.

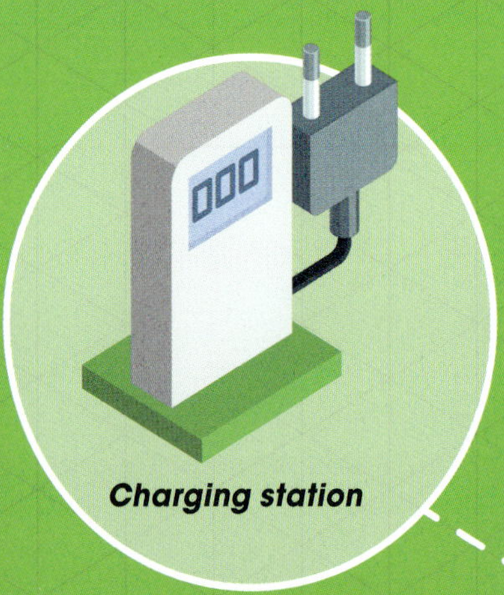

Electric charging

Most electric cars can be charged at home using a normal plug, though it takes several hours. Public fast-charging stations can fill the batteries to 80 percent in about 30 minutes.

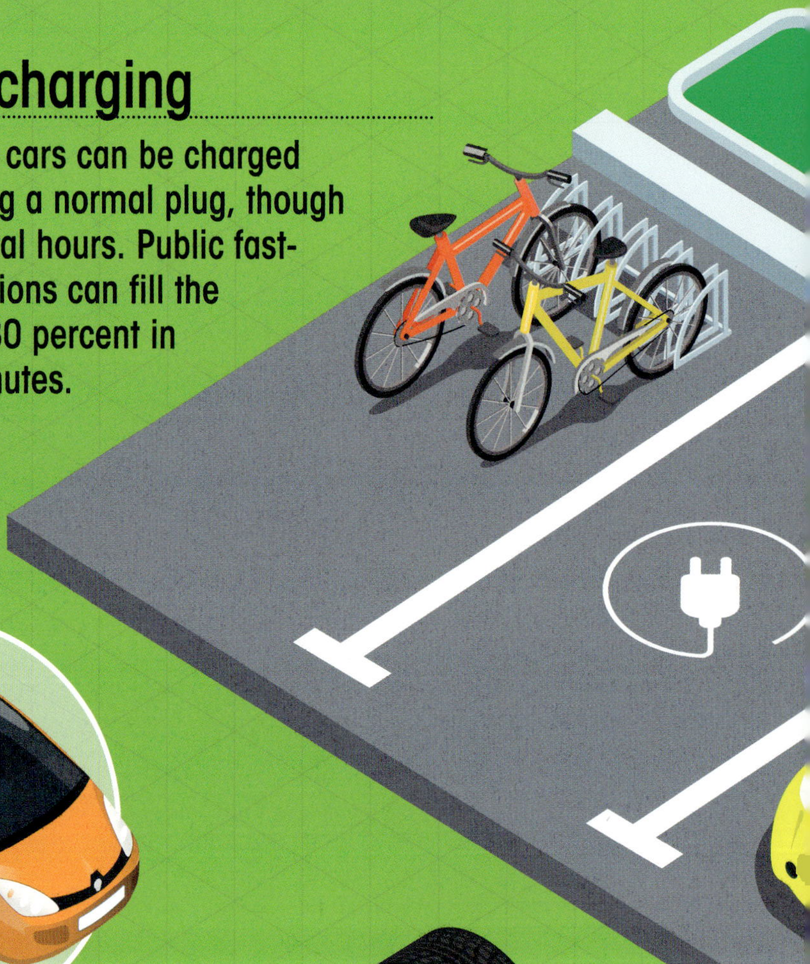

Solar panels

Some cars have their whole roof covered in solar panels. These turn sunlight into electricity, which can be used by the car's power systems

Narrow tires

A car with narrow tires uses less energy because the tires produce less friction against the road surface. However, they also have less grip on the road surface, so cannot be driven as fast.

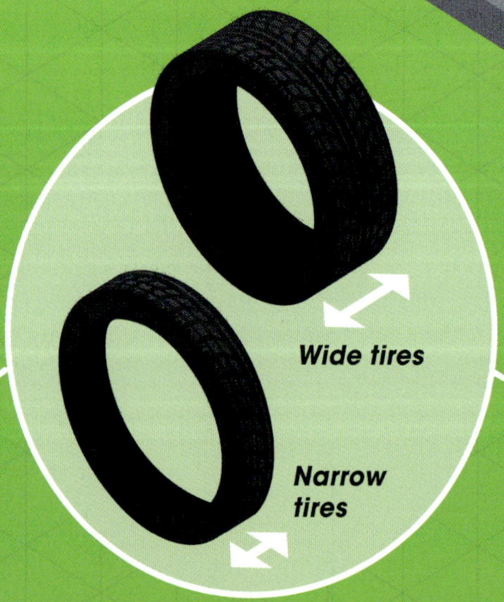

Bicycles

Bicycles are an alternative to electric cars. They produce no pollution, cost less, and can be almost as quick for short journeys – they also help to keep you fit and healthy.

Cycling

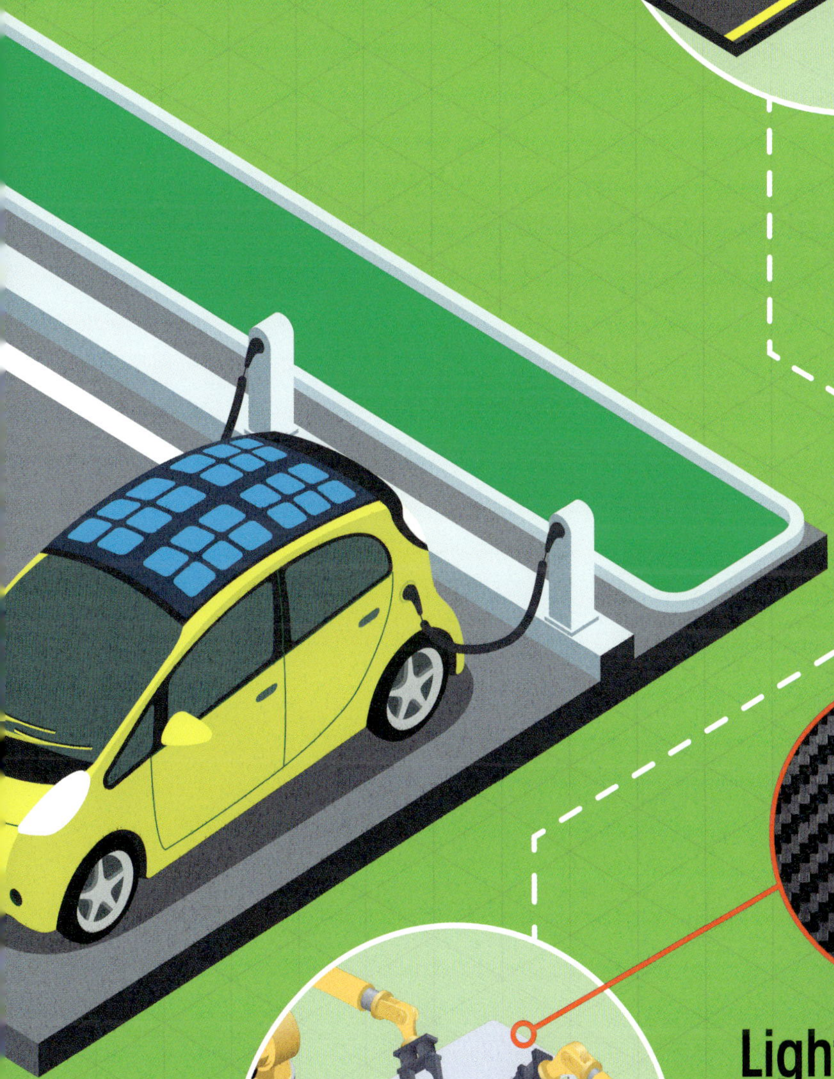

Aerodynamic

An aerodynamic shape is one that pushes easily through the air. This uses less energy, so many electric cars are designed to be aerodynamic.

Carbon fiber is a stronger, lighter alternative to steel.

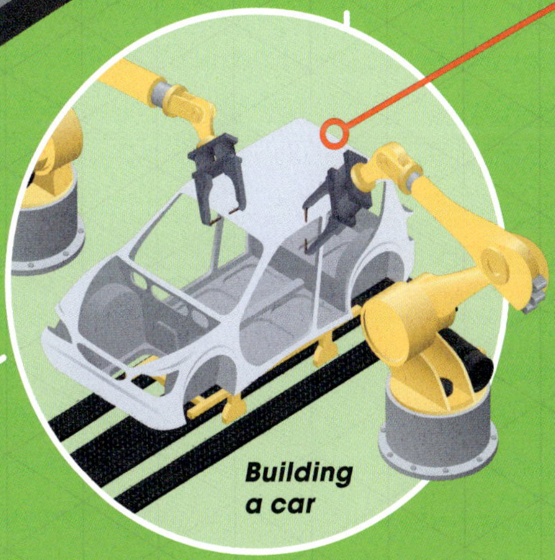

Building a car

Lightweight construction

It is easier to carry a lighter load than a heavy one. The lighter a car can be made, the less energy it will use, so manufacturers use lightweight materials, including aluminium and carbon fiber.

Zero **EMISSIONS**

The harmful gases diesel- and gas-powered vehicles release are called emissions. Today, more and more zero-emissions vehicles are seen on roads and waterways – and even in the skies.

The first electric vehicles

In the 1880s, electric batteries were developed that could hold more electricity than ever before. The first electric vehicles began to appear, including trains, bicycles, and carts. By 1900, London and New York had electric cabs transporting passengers around the city. Electric vehicles started to disappear in the 1910s because gas-powered ones could travel longer distances.

This photograph, taken in 1919, shows an early electric car being charged.

Battery power

Early electric cars could not travel far without having to be recharged. In the 2000s, smaller, more powerful lithium-ion batteries were developed. They made it possible to produce electric-powered vehicles that could travel further and faster than ever before.

72 miles **(117 km)**

2011

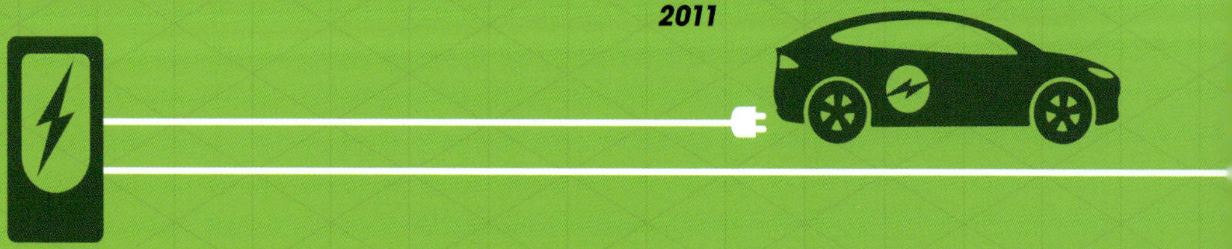

Average distance electric vehicles could travel on one charge.

Bicycles, boats, and aircraft

Today there are electric-powered bikes, boats, and even aircraft. Electric bikes become more popular every year. They have a little electric motor, which adds to the rider's pedaling effort. Electric motors are also being installed in boats: in 2012, the *Pan Solar* became the first solar-electric vehicle to circle the world. And in the air, electric drones and helicopters have been flying since the 2010s. Some companies are even trying to develop electric passenger planes.

Solar Impulse ***is an experimental, solar-powered aircraft that has successfully flown across the U.S. using energy from the sun.***

Solar panels are used to power some boats and ships.

50%

130 million electric bikes were sold worldwide between 2022 and 2023.

More than 368,000 electric bikes were sold in the U.S. in 2021.

368,000

250 miles (400 km)

2023

GLOSSARY

AERODYNAMIC
Something with a shape that allows it to move through air without experiencing a lot of friction.

APP
Short for "application," this is a piece of software that a mobile phone or computer uses to do a particular job.

CARBON EMISSION
Carbon contained in carbon dioxide gas, which is released when oil, coal, or natural gas are burned.

CHECK IN
The process of arriving somewhere - such as an airport, train station, ferry port, or hotel - while traveling.

CLIMATE CHANGE
A long-term warming of Earth's atmosphere caused by human activities such as burning coal and oil.

DATABASE
A list of information held in a computer.

DERAIL
When a train comes off the tracks.

DIESEL
A form of fuel made from petroleum oil.

DOCK
A place in a harbor or shore where ships can load passengers or goods.

FRICTION
The force of resistance created when one object rubs against another.

GEOLOCATION
Finding the exact place someone or something is, using a digital device such as a smartphone.

ICEBREAKER
A special ship that is designed to force its way through icy seas.

INTERACTIVE
Working together.

NETWORK
A group of things or people that are linked together.

PARAMEDIC
A person who is trained to give basic medical help, but who is not a doctor or nurse.

PEDESTRIAN
A person who is walking somewhere.

POLLUTION
A substance that harms the environment.

RADAR
A method of finding ships, planes, and other objects using radio waves. The radio waves are sent out, then bounce back to the sender when they hit something.

SELF-RIGHTING
Able to turn itself back the right way up.

SENSOR
A device that measures physical things. For example, on a car, if low temperatures are detected by a sensor, it might trigger a warning of possible ice on the road.

SURVEILLANCE
Watching, usually without people being aware they are being watched.

TRAFFIC
The number of vehicles, people, or things moving through an area. For example, a road crowded with cars has a lot of traffic.

FOR MORE INFORMATION

PLACES TO VISIT

THE NATIONAL MUSEUM OF TRANSPORTATION
2933 BARRETT STATION ROAD
ST. LOUIS, MO 63122

The National Museum of Transportation has a rail and transit collection of nearly 200 major exhibits. Its collection is recognized as the largest collection of transportation vehicles in the world.

WEBSITE: TNMOT.ORG

NEW YORK TRANSIT MUSEUM
99 SCHERMERHORN STREET
BROOKLYN, NY 11201

The New York Transit Museum is the largest museum in the United States devoted to urban public transportation history.

WEBSITE: NYTRANSITMUSEUM.ORG

SMITHSONIAN NATIONAL AIR AND SPACE MUSEUM
6TH STREET AND INDEPENDENCE AVENUE SW
WASHINGTON, D.C. 20560

Visitors can discover the wonders of air and space by exploring this museum, where they can see artifacts that took humans to new heights. Guest will have an experience that's truly out of this world!

WEBSITE: AIRANDSPACE.SI.EDU

BOOKS TO READ

THE BIG COUNTDOWN: 1.5 BILLION TRANSPORT VEHICLES ON THE WORLD'S ROADS
BEN HUBBARD (Wayland, 2018)
Fascinating facts and numbers about transport, all collected into a very appealing graphic format.

A JOURNEY THROUGH TRANSPORT
CHRIS OXLADE AND JOHN HASLAM (QED, 2017)
Best for those who don't like too much text, this is a fun way to discover the abridged history of transportation, from walking, t to the first cars, and on to supercars and spacecraft.

CARS, TRAINS, SHIPS, AND PLANES: A VISUAL ENCYCLOPEDIA TO EVERY VEHICLE
(Dorling Kindersley, 2015)
They didn't quite manage to fit in every vehicle, but you are likely to find every vehicle you can think of, and a few you can't, in this massive 256-page book.

INDEX